African Safari

Kenya and Tanzania

Jane Moorman

Photographer's Comments

Seeing the animals in the wild is always a thrill, whether they are buffalo in Yellowstone National Park, or elephants in Africa.

While creating a book of bird photographs I had taken on various day trips and vacations, I realized I wanted to take photos of the wild animals in Africa.

I have had a special place in my heart for giraffes since feeding them at the Cheyenne Mountain Zoo in Colorado Springs, Colorado. I wanted to see this majestic animal in the wild.

During the third year of my retirement, I headed to Africa for an 18-day tour of national wildlife reserves in Kenya and Tanzania. Using a Sony RX10iv camera with its built-in 24-600 zoom lens, I took 4,000 photos. I captured photos of 37 different mammals and 42 different birds (featured in my Birds of Africa book).

This book contains the best of the best photos, along with memories and facts about each type of animal. Since the subjects of these photos are breathing, moving animals, I also took video which I have posted on my YouTube website. There are QR Codes in each section and hyperlinks on the last page to take you to those videos, including elephants bathing in a river and a male and female hippo fighting.

Enjoy!

Jane Moorman, photographer

Ambling African Giants

After eating supper, I went to see what was happening outside at the waterhole. We were at the Ark Lodge located in the Aberdare National Park beside a natural watering hole for wild animals.

As I walked into the first-floor observation room, the sight through the floor-to-ceiling windows was unbelievable. A herd of approximately 20 elephants was standing in the spotlit area less than 10 yards away, looking toward the building.

At that moment, I knew this trip was going to be a once-in-a-lifetime experience.

After spending more than an hour watching the herd eat the red, mineral-rich dirt, I was content.

Elephants graze on plants all day long. When they reach an area that has mineral-rich soil, they stop to take in vital nutrients.

Each elephant has one tusk that is a little shorter because it is the one used to dig up the ground so the animal can pick up the dirt with the prehensile fingers at the tip of its trunk and put it in its mouth.

The next morning, I told the tour guide that I could go home now and be very happy. He said, "Just wait. It's going to get better."

Every day while in the national reserves, including the Serengeti, we saw elephants. Usually, they were walking toward some sort of water source — a watering hole, marsh, river, or lake.

The pachyderms, weighing up to six tons, amble along browsing on grass as they move in family units toward water.

One afternoon in the 600-square-mile Maasai Mara National Reserve, we watched the elephants walk into the marsh and sink up to their stomachs before lying down in the water to cool off.

Watching the interaction between the herd members, especially the babies, was fun. You could tell how old the babies were by the length of their trunks. Several times, the trunks were still inches from reaching the ground.

The baby stays close to its mother, sometime even walking under her. When they need a drink of her milk, they raise their head until their trunk flops back and their mouth reaches her two teats located between her front legs. When they are too small for their mouth to reach the teats, they suck their mother's milk into their trunk and then place it in their mouth.

Of all the times of watching the elephants, the last day on the Serengeti was the most memorable. A herd of 31 elephants was coming toward the road we were on.

Our guide said, "Let's just sit here and watch for a while." As they came closer, they had to cross the road in front and behind our truck.

Once across the road, one baby elephant flopped down on the ground, obviously tired. His mother and an older sibling stayed close while he napped, but within minutes, they needed to move on, and he had to get up on his feet, a skill he had not conquered yet.

The guide knew the animals were moving toward a small river. We drove to the other side of the water and waited for the herd to arrive.

First, they took long drinks of the water, filling their trunks and blowing the water into their mouths. Then, they blew water and mud over their bodies to help cool off.

Finally, some rolled in the water. One mother inadvertently backed into her two offsprings, sending one under water. All you could see was the end of its trunk reaching above the water so it could breathe. Soon she moved and it was able to stand.

Follow the QR Code to see video of the baby napping, and the crossing of the small river including the mud baths.

Elephant

Size - Length: 23-29 feet (7-9 m) Height: Male 10-13 feet (3-4 m) Female 8-11 feet (2.4-3.4 m) Weight: Male 8,818–13,889 pounds (4,000-6,300 kg) Female 4,850– 7,716 pounds (2,200-3,500 kg). (2,204 pounds equals 1 ton)

Males have a larger rounded head; tusks are usually larger and thicker than the females'. Female are unique in herbivores in having two teats located between the front legs. Spends most of the day feeding on grass, leaves, bark, fruit and seedpods, constantly moving toward water in either lakes, rivers or marsh areas. The younger the elephant, the shorter its trunk. (left photo) Follow the QR Code to see elephants taking mud bath.

Night Sounds, Dinner Guests

There are a lot of night sounds when you are sleeping in a tent in the Serengeti. The first night at the Embalakai Camp the hyena's high-pitched calls sounded like music all night long.

The second day, an afternoon rain had quieted the hyenas, but they were replaced by a gentle roar, almost like a purr, of a lion.

I was in my tent and really had no concerns about the animal. There weren't screams like something being caught, so I slept comfortably.

The next morning, I asked my fellow travelers if they had heard the lion. No one had. I guess it was a special memory just for me.

The greatest moment of a lion sighting was on the fifth day in the national reserves. We had just finished a sunrise hot air balloon ride and were headed to breakfast when an older male lion walked past our truck, paying no attention to us.

He was majestic with his full mane. He must have seen his fair share of battles during his life because his face had several scares. He was looking for a place to spend a quiet day resting from his night activities.

When we saw lions during the day, they were usually asleep. You almost wondered if they were alive, but with close observation, you could see them breathing.

To conserve energy, they will lie about and rest, sleeping up to 20 hours a day. They do most of their hunting during the cooler part of the day because they do not have many sweat glands.

During our evening drives, we saw three dinner parties.

The first night at the Maasai Mara National Reserve, we were lucky to see a leopard with its catch in a tree and a pride of lions with two freshly caught wildebeest. There were eight young lions present.

I call them parties because the pride of lions share the catch of the day. Each takes a turn eating while the others politely wait.

The next sighting was in the Serengeti in Tanzania. There were four lions enjoying their dinner as we passed by on our way to our lodge.

This encounter demonstrated how the animals are used to the tour trucks and humans. Two lions walked right beside our truck and on down the line of trucks.

A lady in the truck behind us was leaning slightly out of the passenger window, taking a photo with her cell phone. Both lions didn't even react, they just kept walking.

There was a little excitement at the third sighting. A lion was guarding its catch from the hyenas that were closing in wanting to also eat.

There is a ranking of dinner guests at these events: first, the lion, then the hyenas, then the vultures get to clean the remains.

The final big cats sighting was in the Ngorongoro Crater in Tanzania. An older male with full mane was almost camouflaged in the tall brown plants where he was lying.

Follow the QR Code to watch video of the lions in action.

Lion

Mostly hunt in the evening, feeding on Wildebeest, Zebra, Buffalo and Warthog.

Size - Length: Male 5.5-8 feet (172-250 cm) Female 5-6.25 feet (158-192 cm) Tail: 23-39 inches (60-100 cm) Weight: Male 330-573 pounds (150-260 kg) Female 268-401 pounds (122-182 kg)

Leopard

The leopard is among the Big Five Game, along with the lion, elephant, rhinoceros and African buffalo.

It is very rare to see the leopard because they are mostly nocturnal and solitary.

We only saw two from a distance. The first was in the evening, and the cat had carried its prey up into the tree and was resting on the ground beside the tree. The leopard is the only animal that hangs its catch in trees.

They feed on gazelles, impala, warthogs, hares, baboons, monkeys, and birds.

The second one was asleep in a tree a great distance from the road. I was lucky the photo was in focus. I used my 600m lens and enlarged it in the computer.

Size - Length: Male 4.25-76.25 feet (130-190 cm) Female 3.5-4.5 feet (104-140 cm) Tail: 23 inches (60-110 cm) Weight: Male 77-198 pounds (35-90 kg) Female 57-132 pounds (28-60 kg).

Original photo, slightly better than naked eye.

Cheetah

We had two sightings of cheetahs. The first was a mother with three cubs walking down a road toward us.

The second was while the hot air balloon was landing. The cat was headed to bushes nearby. Once in the truck we told the guide where it was, and we went to see how close we could get.

The fastest land animal has been clocked at 33 to 57 mph during a hunt. One stride of a galloping cheetah measures 13 to 22 feet, which increases with speed.

Size - Length: 9-12.5 feet (110-150 c m) Tail: 25-35 inches (65-90 cm) Weight: 77-143 pounds (35-65 kg)

Rare Sighting of Rhinoceros

The first rhino we saw was a good distance from the road. It was lying down and seemed to roll over as we watched.

The next encounter was a group of three white rhinos, including a baby, resting in the shade of a tree. The young rhino was light gray with hardly a horn.

There is no conclusive explanation of the name 'white rhinoceros.' A popular idea that 'white' is a distortion of either the Afrikaans word wyd, or the Dutch word wijd, both meaning wide, referring to the rhino's square lips.

Rhino horns are made of keratin, the same material as hair and fingernails. The horn grows with age.

Poachers kill the animals for their horns, which bring a high price on the black market that is overwhelmingly driven by traditional Chinese medicine. However, there is no good evidence of any health benefits.

Our sighting of the crucially endangered black rhino was in the Serengeti. It was trying to cross the road, but tour trucks were blocking its path.

It ran one direction, but when truck moved into its way, it turned around and ran the other direction. You could tell it was getting mad.

Follow the QR Code to watch the Black Rhino run.

Black Rhinoceros

Both sexes have horns, the front one usually longer. Poor eyesight but good hearing. Generally solitary. It is an odd-toed ungulate with three toes on each foot.

Size - Height: 4.5-5.8 feet (137-180 cm) Length: 9.5-12.25 feet (290-375 cm) Weight: 1,543-3,086 pounds (700-1,400 kg) (2,204 pounds equals 1 ton).

White Rhinoceros

The calf's white-gray coloring darkens with age. Horns grow longer with age.

Size - Height: 5.5-6 feet inches (170-185 cm) Length: 11.75-13.75 feet (360-420 cm) Weight: 4,409-7936 pounds (2,000-3,600 kg)

Cape Buffalo

Size - Height: 3.25-505 feet (100-170 cm) Length: 5.5-11 feet (170-340 cm) Horns: 39 inches (100 cm) Weight: 550-1,874 pounds (250-850 kg). The red-billed oxpecker birds remove bugs off the buffaloes.

The base of Cape buffalo horns comes so close together that they fuse. This creates a shield on their head known as a "boss."

Male's horns are widely curved, with a spread of up to 3 feet wide.

Female's horns are shorter and thinner without a boss. Notice the horns on the female with calf in above photo.

Know Your Giraffe by Its Markings

I have a special place in my heart for giraffes for two reasons. First of all, they are the symbol for an organization called The Giraffe Heroes Project which honors people for sticking their necks out for others.

The second reason is that I had a couple of giraffe figurines, and my mother decided I must be collecting them, so guess what — I now have a sizable collection.

My main desire to go to Kenya was to see giraffes not caged in a zoo. At first, we didn't see many, but by the end of the trip, we saw quite a few.

There are three species of giraffes — Masai, Reticulated and Rothschild's. During a visit to the Giraffe Centre Sanctuary in Nairobi, Kenya, we learned about the markings on the legs that distinguish each species.

We also learned about the work the sanctuary is doing to increase the Rothschild's species back to the wild. They are breeding the animals and releasing the two-year olds into Lake Nakuru National Park after acclimating them to self-survive.

Masai giraffes are fawn-colored with variable star-shaped, blotched markings, which darken with age. They have markings on the entire length of their legs.

Males are larger than females, with two thick horns, which are bald at the tips, and a smaller horn on the forehead. Female's horns are covered by long hair.

Reticulated giraffes have dark, chestnut-colored square patches outlined with fine white lines. They have markings down the front of their lower legs.

Rothschild's giraffes have no markings below their knees. The male also differs in having five horns rather than three.

Giraffe horns are not true horns but bone protuberances fused in the skull.

To eat, they use their prehensile lip and 17-inch-long tongues to browse on leaves and twigs up to 19.5 feet above ground.

The males spar, sometimes called necking, with one another for dominance. They stand shoulder to shoulder and swing their heads at one another like a club.

Giraffes are not mute but make grunts and braying distress calls. They defend themselves and their young by kicking with their forelegs.

When giraffes walk, their front and back legs on the same side move forward together. Follow the QR Code to watch the giraffe walk.

A group of giraffes is identified as a journey or tower, not as a herd.

Sizes for each specie is as follows:

Masia: Height: Male 12-17 feet (3.9-5.2 m) Female: 11-15 feet (3.5-4.7 m) Length: 11.5-15.75 feet (3.5-4.8 m) Tail: 30-43 inches (76-110 cm) Weight: Male 3,968-4,255 pounds (1800-1930 kg) Female 992-2,601 pounds (450-1,180 kg)

Reticulated: Height: 14.75-16.5 feet (4.5-5 m) Length: 11.5-15-75 feet (3.5-4.8 m) Tail: 29-43 inches (76-110 cm) Weight: Male 3,968-4,255 pounds (1,800-1930 kg) Female 992-2,601 pounds (450-1,180 kg).

Rothschild's: Height: 14.75-18 feet (4.5-5.5 m) Length 110-15.75 feet (3.5-4.8 m) Tail 30-40 inches (76-110 cm) Weight: Male 3,968-4,255 pounds (1800-1930 kg) Female 992-2,601 pounds (450-1,180 kg).

Giraffe

Male Rothschild's Giraffes

Female Masia Giraffes

Male Masia Giraffe

Male Rothschild's Giraffe

Female Masia Giraffe with young female

Male Reticulated Giraffes journey

Special Baboon Encounter

My first encounter with a baboon was a very special moment. I was walking along a bridge at The Ark Lodge in the Aberdare National Park when I came upon a mother baboon with her baby nursing.

The sunlight through the mother's fur gave a golden halo around the pair.

The male baboon was close by, keeping an eye on me. He gave a cry letting me know not to get any closer, then he moved to a position between myself and the mother and baby. The trio jumped off the bridge and reappeared farther down the path.

The primates and I were on the bridge for an evening ritual when the lodge employee brought a tray of cubed fruit out to attract birds for the guests to photograph.

Once the tray was hung, to the surprise of the people, the male baboon leaped onto it to take some fruit before jumping down to the ground below the bridge.

We saw several troops of baboons during our travel. They were usually on the move with the youth either running along to keep up or getting a ride on a parent's back.

The dominate male was usually bringing up the rear of the group, walking with his tail in an upright, curved position when walking. Females carry their newborn under the belly, and after six weeks, the baby rides on their parent's back.

Follow the QR Code to watch the baboon parade.

Olive Baboon

Males hold their tails in an upright, curved position when walking. Females carry their newborn under the belly; at about six weeks, they ride on their parent's back.

 Size - Length: 4-4.5 feet (127-142 cm) Tail: 17-26 inches (45- 68) Weight: Male: 48-66 pounds (22-30 kg) Female: 24-66 pounds (11-30 kg).

Beware: Wildlife Nearby

The evening entertainment at the lodges was provided by the wildlife that wandered through the property. Zebras, waterbuck and even giraffes were frequent visitors to the resort properties.

During each lodge check-in we were told to have an escort guide when going to and from the main lodge to our room or tent.

While this seemed to be a hassle, it was for our own protection. The guide would carry a powerful flashlight to shine into shadows to be sure a visiting animal was not nearby.

During my morning walk to breakfast at the Lake Naivasha Sopa Resort, I had to stop and take photos of the animals lounging in the yard.

There was concern at this resort because the property extends to the shore of the lake, where hippos live. Hippos leave the water at night to graze and are very dangerous if you encounter them.

One evening, two zebras were nibbling on the flower bush outside my room. I was able to walk near them. Further down the sidewalk, a group of waterbucks were playing in the yard.

The zebra was more interested in eating than saying hello to me. Follow the QR Code to watch the waterbucks playing.

Monkey Business

"Keep your balcony door closed" was a common direction from lodge personnel. There was wildlife in the area including monkeys. Monkeys are very curious animals, including entering open balcony doors.

Eastern Black and White Colobus

The Eastern Black and White Colobus, specifically the Mantled Guereza, was a resident of the Lake Naivasha Sopa Resort. It sat in the trees near the lodge.

The word "colobus" comes from Greek for mutilated, because unlike other monkeys, colobus monkeys do not have thumbs.

The Colobus' beautiful black fur strongly contrasts with the long white mantle, whiskers, bushy tail, and beard around the face. The Eastern black-and-white is distinguished by a U-shaped cape of white hair running from the shoulders to lower back.

Vervet Monkey

The vervet is a small, black-faced monkey, common in East Africa.

The body is a greenish-olive or silvery gray. The face, ears, hands, feet, and tip of the tail are black, but a conspicuous white band on the forehead blends in with the short whiskers. The arms and legs are approximately equal length.

Vervets living near areas inhabited by people can become pests stealing food and other items and raiding crops.

Size - Length: 21–25 inches (54-65 cm) Tail: 25-35 inches (65-90 cm) Weight: 22-50 pounds (10-23 kg)

Vervet Monkey

Notice the red eye of the monkey in the right photo. It is not normal, so the animal is having some type of vision problem, maybe blindness.

Size - Length: Male 19-25 inches (50-65 cm) Female 14-24 inches (38-62 cm) Weight: Male 8-17 pounds (4-8 kg) Female 7-11 pounds (3.5-5 kg). Feed on bark, flowers, fruit, grass seeds, bird eggs and nestlings.

Hippos: Sleeping Giants

The first hippopotamus we saw looked like rocks in the water. Then we saw some lying on a rock out of the water, motionless, sleeping. In this drowsy state, a few would open their eyes and look at us as our boat passed.

During the day, the third largest living land mammal remains cool by staying in the water or mud. Their eyes, ears and nostrils are placed high on the roof of their skulls. This allows them to be mostly submerged.

They need to be submerged because their thin, naked skin is vulnerable to overheating and dehydration.

One evening, on the way back to camp, the driver took a route past a waterhole filled with hippos. We knew they were in the area because of the smell of the stagnant water.

Dominate hippo males mark their territory with their dung. The effective scent warns off other male hippos who might try to invade his territory.

Hippos live in herds, called pods, of 10-40 individuals. The pod we saw could have been easily 30 animals.

The hippos were beginning to stir from their naps. As we watched, one would raise its head and open its mouth wide, then another, and another. Others were swishing their tails back and forth.

They were slowly waking for their nocturnal activity of emerging from the water to graze on grass. They can consume around 100 pounds of grass in one night.

After grazing most of the night, before sunrise, they head back into the water to digest their food and to spend another day lazing beneath the water's surface.

While driving through the Ngorongoro Crater, a volcanic caldron that covers 100 square miles, we saw a bull hippo and a mother hippo with two calves, probably her last two calves with one still small, in a marsh area.

Calves stay close to their mother for protection, not only from crocodiles and lions but from male hippos who attack young males in the water.

At first, I thought it was a family, but then the bull started attaching the female, known as a cow.

This was the first time our guide had seen a hippo fight between a bull and a cow. He said he once saw two males fight.

If a male hippo comes near the young, a mother hippo will attack him. We watched in awe as the mother stood her ground against the bull.

He opened his mouth to a massive 150 degrees, approximately four feet wide, showing his large tusk-like canines and razor-sharp incisors teeth.

The cow responded by moving between the bull and her young. She faced the aggressive male with the defensive action of an open mouth.

She also moved her head back-and-forth scooping muddy water into the male's mouth and face when he postured with an open mouth. The adults also charged each other.

The male ran a good distance away after the mother's first charge. She moved back into a protective position, appearing to think the male would leave, but he didn't. He charged back, and the posturing, grunting and roaring resumed.

There was one more short charge from each fighter, and then the male retreated, walking in a submissive gait.

It is unsure why the male hippo attacked. We knew we just had a once-in-a-lifetime experience.

Hippopotamus
"Hippos"

Hippo Fight

Male and female hippos fighting as the mother is protecting her calves. See the entire fight by using the QR Code.

Size - Height: 4.25-5.3 feet (130-165 cm) Length: 10.25-13.75 feet (320-420 cm) Weight: Male 1,433-7,054 pounds (650-3,200 kg) Female 1,124-5,511 pounds (510-2,500 kg). (2,204 pounds equals 1 ton)

See more video of hippos by following this QR Code.

Warthog

Two characteristics of warthogs that make them fun to watch are how they kneel to eat and when they run, their tail is straight up with a tuft of hair on the end.

When they ran, it was too quick for me to get a photo. They can run at speeds up to 30 mph.

They are so prevalent that you get to a place of saying, "Just another warthog."

A member of the pig species, the warthog has adapted to grazing and savanna habitats.

Not having a flexible neck, they have adapted to graze short grasses by being able to lower themselves close to the ground on their wrist joints. They look like they are praying.

The two pairs of tusks protruding from the mouth and curving upward are used for digging, fighting and in defense against predators.

The lower, shorter pair of tusks become razor-sharp by rubbing against the upper pair each time the mouth is opened and closed.

Short hair covers most of their bodies. There is longer hair on a mane that goes down the spine to the middle of the back.

Their name is derived from patches on their faces that look like warts. There are three different facial warts, with the suborbital growing as long as six inches (15 cm) in males.

The animal's social groups are called sounders, which can contain up to 18 individuals. Females live in these groups with their young, while the males leave their natal group at around two years old. Females only leave sounders when they are pregnant.

Warthogs have poor eyesight, but their hearing and sense of smell are very good.

They are not fighters and are much more likely to flee from larger predators, such as lions.

Size - Height: 21-33 inches (55-85 cm) Length: 41-60 inches (105-152 cm) Weight: Male 132-330 pounds (60-150 kg) Female 99-165 pounds (45-75 kg)

Zebras, Wildebeest: Symbiotic Relationship

The first question that comes to mind when you see a zebra is, "Is it white with black stripes or black with white stripes?"

At first glance, it may appear the opposite is true — after all, the black stripes of many zebras end on the belly and toward the inside of the legs, revealing the rest as white. But looks are deceiving in the zebra's case.

Beneath all that fur, zebras have black skin. A shaved zebra, without any stripes, could be almost unrecognizable as an all-black animal.

The melanocyte cells in the fur follicles are responsible for generating melanin, the pigment that gives color to skin and hair.

For zebras, chemical messengers determine which melanocytes deliver pigment to which sections of fur, thus creating the zebra's black-and-white pattern.

The white fur represents an absence of melanin; white is not its own pigment.

The stripe pattern is like a human's fingerprint — each zebra has its own pattern.

The other question that arises is: Is a zebra a horse? The answer is yes. Zebras were the second species to diverge from the earliest proto-horses after the asses.

Besides their stripes, the zebra differs from horses with manes made of short, erect hair and tails tufted at the tip.

Wildebeests and zebras have a symbiotic relationship for many reasons. One is that they can graze in the same areas. The zebra eats the long, tough grasses, while the wildebeest feeds upon shorter, softer grass and succulent plants.

They need each other during the migration: wildebeest are good at finding water sources and zebras know the way of the migration.

Zebras have a keen sense of sight, which allows them to spot any potential threats from a distance. On the other hand, wildebeests have excellent hearing and sense of smell, which helps them detect predators that may be lurking nearby. The wildebeests' sense of smell also helps the animals find water to drink.

A group of wildebeests is called a confusion, which could describe their behavior when they start running.

Zebras see potential danger and start to run away from it. The wildebeests will start to run as well, but at a short distance, they may stop and wonder: what are we running from? Both animals can run at speeds up to 40 miles per hour.

The wildebeest is one of the most abundant large mammals in Africa. There are thought to be around 1.5 million migratory individuals in the Serengeti alone forming the greatest concentration of wild grazing animals on Earth.

During the Great Migration, the herds travel a total of 500 miles, during each cycle. The zebras have a great memory and are able to recall safe migration routes, which helps guide the sometimes-aimless wildebeests.

The Serengeti in Tanzania is a vast, flat pasture. It is in this environment that the animals give birth to their young during January and February. The wide-open terrain allows the animals to see predators approaching.

Zebra

Size - Height: 4-4.5 feet (127-140 cm) Length: 7-8 feet (217-246 cm) Weight: Male 485-709 pounds (220-322 kg) Female 385-551 pounds (175-250 kg).

Zebras stay in family groups that consist of one stallion, a few mares, and their young ones.

Newborn foals have a mane down the back to the tail and are brown, black and white. The foals begin to change to adult coloration after four months.

Zebras, like horses, enjoy a good roll in the dirt and a good tree rub.

Follow the QR Code to watch the zebras.

View From Above

Follow the QR Code to watch the zebras and wildebeest move across the Sarangani in videos taken from a sunrise hot air balloon ride.

Antelopes

Africa has more antelopes than any other continent. There are 72 antelope species in Africa, with only 16 different antelopes in the Serengeti National Park. They are identified by their fur markings and horns.

We saw 12 different species during the two-week safari, including Wildebeest, Gerenuk, Topi, Dik-Dik, Impala, Hartebeest, Bushbuck, Waterbuck, Thomson's gazelle, Grant's gazelle, Reedbuck and Giant kudu.

The most prevalent are the wildebeests, impalas, and Thomson's gazelles.

Wildebeests have a black marking from the base of their horns to the nose. The ungainly gnu pronounced "g-new" or simply "new" earned the Afrikaans name wildebeest, or "wild beast," for the menacing appearance presented by its large head, shaggy mane, pointed beard and sharp curved horns.

The impalas and gazelles look similar until you study their markings. The impala is identified by the black markings of its rump and tail that form an "M."

While the gazelle also has a white rump, its black marking is on the outside edge of the white, as well as no black marking on the tail. It is distinguishable from the impala by the broad black band on its side.

During the safari, the smallest antelope spotted was the Kirk's dik-dik. They may only stand 13-18 inches high, but they are fast, reaching speeds up to 26 miles per hour (42 km/hour).

The Gerenuk have giraffe-like necks to feed from branches others can't reach.

The most elegant antelope species include the Kudu, Impala, Waterbuck, Gerenuk, and Bushbuck.

Antelopes are one of the primary food sources for Africa's large predators, including lions, leopards and even crocodiles.

Although antelopes are sometimes referred to and easily misidentified as deer, true deer are only distantly related to antelope. Only one deer species is found in Africa—the Barbary red deer of Northern Africa.

Unlike deer, in which the males sport elaborate head antlers that are shed and regrown annually, antelope horns are bone and grow steadily, never falling off. If a horn is broken, it will either remain broken or take years to partially regenerate, depending on the species.

The size and shape of horns varies greatly. They range from twisted, spiral and recurved to lyrate or long, curved horns.

Horns are efficient weapons and tend to be better developed in those species where males fight over females than in solitary species.

In male competitions, horns are clashed in combat. Males more commonly use their horns against each other than against other species.

The boss, or base where the horns are attached to the head, is typically arranged in such a way that two antelope striking at each other's horns cannot crack each other's skulls, making a fight via horn more ritualized than dangerous.

Another trait of antelopes is the placement of their eyes on the sides of their heads, giving them a broad radius of vision.

Watch the young Grant's Gazelles practice fighting at the following QR Code.

Blue, White-Beard Wildebeest

As wildebeest age, their horns expand, spreading horizontally from the base and curving inward to the point. Above photo young calf compared to older on left.

Size - Height: 3.8-4 feet (117-123 cm) Length: 5.5-7.8 feet (170-240 cm) Horns: 18-30 inches (45-76 cm) Weight: Male 440 pounds (200 kg) Female 360 pounds (163 kg).

Common waterbuck

Distinguishing marks: white rump, bib, muzzle and eyebrows. Grazes mostly but browses during dry season. Size - Height: 47-53-5 inches (120-136 cm) Length: 69.5-92.5 inches (177-235 cm) Horns: Male only 21.5-39 inches (55-99 cm) Weight: Male 441-661 pounds (200-300 kg) Female 353-441 pounds (160-200 kg).

Giant Kudu

They are browsers feeding on herbs and flowers on vines.

Size - Height: Male 4-5 feet (122-150 cm) Female 3.25-4.5 feet (100-140 cm) Length: Male 6.3-8 feet (195-245 cm) Female 6-7.5 feet (185-235 cm) Horns: Male only 4 feet (120 cm) Weight: Male 419-694 pounds (190-315 kg) Female 264.5-474 pounds (120-215 kg).

Coke's Hartebeest

Size - Height: 3.5-4.9 feet (107-150 cm) Length: 5.25-8 feet (160-245 cm) Horns: 18-32.5 inches (45-83 cm) Weight: Male 275.5-480 pounds (125-218 kg) Female 255-407 pounds (116-185 kg).

Distinguishing marking: A large, long-faced, uniformly fawn-colored with a pale rump. Has high, humped shoulders and long, slim legs. Both sexes have horns, which are short and thick, diverging almost horizontally at the base before turning upwards and backwards.

Cape Bushbuck

Distinguishing mark: Black ban around the base of the neck.

The male becomes darker, almost black, with age; has short spiral horns.

Solitary, except when a female has young. Grazer and browser.

Size - Height: 24-39 inches (61-100 cm) Length: 41-59 inches (105-150 cm) Horns: Males only 9-10.5 inches (25-27 cm) Weight: Male 66-176 pounds (30-80 kg) Female 53-132 pounds (24-60 kg)

Topi

Size - Height: 3.4-4 feet (104-126 cm) Length: 5-7.5 feet (150-230 cm) Horns: 5-6 feet (150-180 cm) Weight: Male 265-353 pounds120-160 kg) Female 165-339 pounds (75-150 kg). Distinguishing black face.

Grant's Gazelle

Distinguishing marks: Long legs, white rump which extends above white tail. Females have a faint dark stripe along their flank. Both sexes have horns. Males' horns are larger and graceful, extending upward and outward.

Size - Height: Male 33.5-36 inches (85-91 cm) Female 30.7-32.5 inches (78-83 cm) Length: 55-65 inches (140-166 cm) Horns: 19.5-31.5 inches (50-80 cm) Weight: Male 132-178.5 pounds (60-81 kg) Female 83.75-148 pounds (38-67 kg)

Follow the QR Code to see young males sparing on video.

Impala

Distinguishing marks: Rump is white with a black line on either side and tail has black line, which creates an M so it is easy to identify impalas.

Male horns have widespread S-shaped horns.

Above left photo: Male with one broken horn. Right photo: Mother with calf nursing.

Size - Height: 29.5-37 inches (75-95 cm) Length: 47– 63 inches (120-160 cm) Horns: Male only 18-36 inches (45-92 cm) Weight: Male 99-176 pounds (45-80 kg) Female 88-132 pounds (40-60 kg)

Thomson's Gazelle

Distinguishing marks: Broad black band on side. Rump white up to root of tail, bordered by black. Short distance between ridged horns.

Grazer, but browses in the dry season.

Size - Height: 21.5-32 inches (55-82 cm) Length: 31.5-47 inches (80-120 cm) Horns: 27.5-40 inches (70-102 cm) Weight: Male 44-77 pounds (20-35 kg) Female 33-55 pounds (15-25 kg)

Gerenuk

Can stand erect on its hindlegs and, with its long neck extended, browse on tall bushes. At times, uses its front legs to pull down higher branches. Does not require water and rarely drinks.

Distinguishing marks: Darker brown along the back.

Size - Height: 31.5-41 inches (80-105 cm) Length: 55-63 inches (140-160 cm) Horns: Male only 12.5-17 inches (32-44) Weight: Male 68-115 pounds (31-52 kg) Female 62-99 pounds (28-45 kg).

Kirk's dik-dik

A small, delicate-looking antelope with an elongated, almost trunk like nose. The tuft of hair on the crown is raised in alarm. Large ears, large, white-rimmed eyes and distinct preorbital glands.

Size - Height: 13-18 inches (35-45 cm) Length: 21-28 inches (55-72 cm) Horns: Male only 3-4 inches (8-11 cm) Weight: 8-16 pounds (3.8-7.2 kg)

Chanler's Mountain Reedbuck

Distinct bark blackish patch beneath ears. Mostly a grazer, but also browses in dry season.
Size - Height: 23–31 inches (60-80 cm) Length: 43-53 inches (110-136 cm) Horns: Males only 5.5-6.75 inches (14-17 cm) Weight: Male 48.5-83 pounds (22-38 kg) Female 42-77 pounds (19-35 kg).

Repile - Red-headed Rock Agama

   Distinguishing marks: Male has a bright orange head and blue body. Females are mottled brown with rufous patches, dark marks across the body and speckles of green on the head. Female lays 4-9 eggs. Males usually seen basking on rocks or displaying by bobbing the head up and down.
   Size - Length: Up to 13.5 inches (35 cm)

Silver-backed Jackal

Feeds on almost anything. Rarely scavenges.
 Size - Length: 33-37 inches (86-96 cm) Height: 27-31inches (70-80 cm) Tail: 14–17 inches (35-45 cm)
Weight: 16-44 pounds (7.3-20 kg)

Bush Hyrax

Feeds on leaves, particularly Acacia tortilis, but also on fruits, twigs, and bark.
Size - Length: 12.5–22 inches (32-57 cm) Weight: 4-8 pounds (2-3.5 kg)

Scavengers: The Clean-up Crew

Hyenas, vultures, and crocodiles are the clean-up crew for the African ecosystem.

Lions are the apex predators and keystone predators, meaning they initiate the food chain by killing mostly wildebeest, zebras and antelopes.

After they have eaten their fill, the "clean-up" takes over.

Hyenas and crocodiles, if killing is near water, are usually the first to dine, followed by the vultures that pick the bones clean.

As we drove toward a river crossing in the Maasai Mara National Reserve in Kenya, our driver saw vultures circling in the sky. He said, "Those birds circling is called a 'kettle.' Something's happening over there. Let's go see what's up."

We followed the dirt roads until we were near the vultures gathering on the remains of a carcass. Soon, a large group, known as a venue, had gathered, causing fights while individuals tried to get a better position at the meal.

There are eight species of vultures in Africa. The birds have incredible eyesight during the day, which enables them to spot a carcass from around four miles away.

In the Serengeti, we saw two hyenas approach a lion while it was still eating, which caused the lion to give them a warning growl to stay away.

The next-to-last night at the tent camp on the Serengeti, the man escorting me to my tent told me the sounds we were hearing were the hyenas.

It wasn't a laugh but more of a high-pitched whining and whooping. It was very musical and lasted most of the night.

Follow the QR Code to watch the vultures gather for a clean-up meal.

Spotted Hyena

Spots fade with age. Scavenger. Skillful hunters, killing Wildebeest calves.
Size - Length: 3.25-5.8 feet (100-180 cm) Tail: 9-14 inches (25-36 cm) Weight: 88-198 pounds (40-90 kg)

Lappet-face Vulture

The combination of the dull red or pink head and fleshy folds on the side of it are distinctive of this species. Length: 37-45 inches (95-115 cm) with a wingspan of 8.2-9.5 feet (2.5-2.9 m).

Ruppell's Griffon Vulture

Distinguished by a creamy-white edging in the body and wing feathers, which gives it a scaly appearance. The head and almost-bare neck are grey with sparse, whitish down. The bill is horn-colored, tinged pink. Length: 37-42 inches (95-107 cm)

White Backed Vulture

A large, uniformly brown vulture with a long, almost bare neck with a pale ruff at its base. The white back and rump are seen only in flight. Immature distinguished from immature Ruppell's Vulture by its darker appearance and shorter bill. Length: 35-38.5inches (89-98 cm)

Marabou Stork

When sitting, legs hinge forwards, compared to humans. A scavenger, but also feeds on rodents and insects. An extendable pink air sac hangs down from the base of the neck. Length: 59 inches (152 cm)

Nile Crocodile

Nile Crocodiles live in rivers, lakes, and dams. A swift swimmer but can move fast on land, too. Able to stay underwater for up to 45 minutes. Carnivorous hunting fish and mammals in the water will also snatch humans and other mammals on the water's edge.

Size - Length: up to 18 feet (5.5 m) Weight: up to 2,204 pounds (1,000 kg)

YouTube video links

Elephant videos
Baby elephant getting up from a nap: Https://youtu.be/T8ClypF5Euw
Elephant herd in the Serengeti, Tanzania: Https://youtu.be/0U9yFhErVdk
Elephant herd crossing a river: Https://youtu.be/EqW93RDNOtc
Elephants visit waterhole at night: (22:17): Https://youtu.be/DrTxq2mkVMY
Elephant and hyena: Https://youtu.be/zxgJq6h_uM0

Wildebeest video
Wildebeest on the move: Https://youtu.be/8k8G3f-omtl

Hippo videos
Hippo pod in river: Https://youtu.be/N_qLYiYABMI
Hippo fight: Https://youtu.be/RDA-v_rPZjw

Waterbucks video
Waterbucks at Lake Naivasha Sopa Lodge: Https://youtu.be/6opkVlMNMvs

Baboons video
Baboons along the road: Https://youtu.be/ap6g4zf9PKA

Giraffes video
Giraffes in the Maasai Mara in Kenya: Https://youtu.be/LTIs_AhhrRk

Lion videos
Lion with humans: Https://youtu.be/cqIoBBR9iww
Male lion walking: Https://youtu.be/eZfLsFHsNdQ
Lion diner party: Https://youtu.be/BpSduzzHu68

Rhino video
Black rhino running: Https://youtu.be/j8CL6-tA2IgY

Gazelle's video
Gazelles practice fighting: Https://youtu.be/iOg2lBLd9-RU

Zebras video
Zebras: Https://youtu.be/x-M5620Bl7g

Vultures video
Vultures dining: Https://youtu.be/Xd8MPu7a1WU

About the Photographer

Jane Moorman describes herself as an adventurer who loves to drive the backroads to see what there is to see.

During her 30-year journalism career, Jane honed her photographic skills as a photojournalist, including covering high school sporting events.

A friend once said, "I wish I could see the world as Jane sees it. Finding the beauty in things that most of us don't take time to see."

Upon retiring in 2021, Jane decided there was a lot of her native country she had not visited, including each state's capitol, so she began her journey of exploring the USA.

In 2023, Jane visited two places on her bucket list — Kenya for an African Safari and Switzerland to see the Alps.

She currently lives in Albuquerque, New Mexico, but says her real home is on the road.

When she is not on the road, she is at home building photo books of what she has seen.

She currently has published books on the Great Lake Lighthouses and United States state capitols, as well as other interesting things she has discovered during her travels.

Other books in the works include Switzerland by Train: visiting three mountains by cog trains, and the United States east and west coast lighthouses.

Her books are available on Amazon.com and other digital book platforms.

Acknowledgement

Information regarding the length and weight of the animals if from *"Wildlife of East Africa: A photographic Guide,"* by Dave Richards. Published by Struik Nature, Random House Struik Ltd.